SCRIPTURE MEN

Knowin

Middle School
Key Stage 3

SCRIPTURE MEMORY PROGRAM

Knowing God

Prepared by
N.A. Woychuk, M.A., Th.D.

CF4•K

10 9 8 7 6 5 4 3 2 1
© Copyright 2012 N.A. Woychuk

ISBN: 978-1-84550-779-4

Published in 2012 by
Christian Focus Publications,
Geanies House, Fearn, Tain
Ross-shire, IV20 1TW, U.K.

Cover design by Daniel van Straaten
Ilustrations by Fred Apps
Printed and bound by Bell and Bain, Glasgow

The Scripture versions used throughout this book are The King James and the English Standard Version.

Contents

INTRODUCTION

This book is a Scripture memory book aimed at young people who are in Middle School in the United States or who are at Key Stage 3 in the United Kingdom. The age range would be approximately eleven years old and above.

In this book, we have eighty-four verses of Scripture arranged carefully under twelve meaningful assignment headings. As you memorize these passages of God's Word, you will be studying the great truths concerning God Himself.

The verses come in the King James Version and also in the English Standard Version. The notes are based on the King James. The two versions are similar. In counsel with your parents and advisors, you decide which version you will memorize. You must stick with the same version all the way through.

The preface pages give a little summary about the meaning of each assignment. The helps and explanations, which are provided with each assignment, will help you to understand the passage of Scripture. It is always much easier to memorize God's Word when you really understand it. Learn to pronounce the words correctly.

The art illustrations, poems, etc., are included so as to make the Memory book more attractive and enjoyable for you.

Be sure to study carefully the "Rules for Memorizing" and "Countdown for Happy Memorizing" given in the next few pages. God bless you as you study and memorize His precious Word (Jeremiah 15:16).

N.A.W.

RULES FOR MEMORIZING

1. Memorize the name of your memory book and the assignment headings in the order given.

2. Memorize the Bible references as printed with each verse or group of verses.

3. Memorize the verses exactly as they are printed. Do not add, do not change and do not leave out any words.

4. Of course, you do not memorize the introduction to each assignment, nor the helps and explanations.

5. In reciting you will give the name of the Book, the heading, the reference, then the verse or verses under that reference, just as printed.

6. You are required to learn the verses during the first part of the week. You will not be doing acceptable work if you wait until the latter part of the week to begin memorizing, no matter how smart you are.

7. You are not allowed to recite just part of an assignment. You must recite an entire assignment at one time.

8. You are permitted to recite more than one assignment on the first recitation day, but after that, you may recite only one assignment a week, as we definitely require that you spend the whole week preparing each assignment.

9. You must memorize well. You should never have to be prompted. It is a poor recitation if you have to be prompted more than four times. For such a recitation you get a check. This tells you that you must try to do much better the next week.

    By "prompting" we mean drawing attention to a mistake and helping you to recollect and to get the connection in the verses, which means if absolutely necessary two or three words may be suggested; but when you have to be told several words or a sentence, it is obvious you are not prepared.

10. Failing to know one assignment may disqualify you as your hearer may decide.

11. You are to recite at a set time and place each week.

COUNTDOWN TO HAPPY MEMORIZING

10. Ask God to help you. You have begun a great adventure with the Lord.

9. Read the whole assignment through carefully. Notice how each verse relates to the assignment heading.

8. Look up the verses in your Bible and read the passages where the verses are found. This will help you understand the thought and remember the references.

7. Study the "Helps and Explanations" so that you will know and understand the meaning of the verses.

6. Find a quiet corner for yourself. When you memorize, you must concentrate and put your whole mind on your work.

5. Relax. Don't be hurried. Plan to spend enough time each day so that you can enjoy the Word of God and let God speak to your heart through it. God will help you if you do your very best.

4. Keep your goal in sight – a perfect recitation. Do not allow yourself to be content with even the smallest mistakes. "Get tough" with yourself – it's good training.

3. Set up your time-schedule for the week as the rules direct, beginning your memorizing on Saturday and Sunday, with a verse or two on Monday. The rest of the week is spent in review, repeating the verses over and over, using them in prayer, in conversation and in writing.

2. Arrange for members of your family or some of your friends to follow in the Book and check you as you review for your recitation.

1. GO! Remember God's Word can take you higher than any rocket has ever been – right into the presence of God.

O GOD, OUR HELP IN AGES PAST

O God, our help in ages past,
Our hope for years to come;
Our shelter from the stormy blast,
And our eternal home.

Under the shadow of Thy throne
Thy saints have dwelt secure;
Sufficient is Thine arm alone,
And our defense is sure.

Before the hills in order stood,
Or earth received her frame,
From everlasting Thou art God,
To endless years the same.

A thousand ages in Thy sight
Are like an evening gone;
Short as the watch that ends the night
Before the rising sun.

O God, our help in ages past,
Our hope for years to come;
Be Thou our guard while life shall last,
And our eternal home.

Isaac Watts

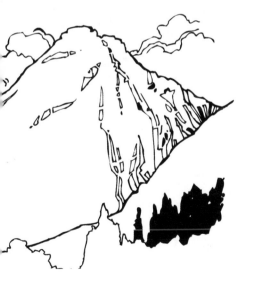

KNOWING GOD AS ETERNAL

PREFACE – ASSIGNMENT 1

God always has been. God the Father, God the Son and God the Holy Spirit had no beginning and will have no ending.

All other things which we know or have heard about had a beginning, and most things come to an end. God is greater than anything else we know in the world. He is not controlled by time in any way. We may not understand how this can be, yet we know it is true, for the Bible tells us so.

The adult Mayfly lives about 24 hours. Suppose two Mayflies were talking one day: "I cannot believe that boys and girls could live as long as sixty or seventy years," says one, "nobody in our family ever lived that long."

"How could such a thing be possible?" the other one remarked. "None of us has ever lived that long, so I do not believe that boys or girls do either."

Just because the Mayfly cannot understand the span of human life does not make it any less true. Neither does it change the fact that God is eternal just because some human beings cannot understand it or will not believe it.

KING JAMES VERSION
ASSIGNMENT 1
KNOWING GOD AS ETERNAL

Job 36:26

Behold, God is great, and we know him not,

neither can the number of his years be searched out.

Psalm 90:2

Before the mountains were brought forth,

or ever thou hadst formed the earth and the world,

even from everlasting to everlasting,

thou art God.

Isaiah 46:9, 10

Remember the former things of old:

for I am God, and there is none else; I am God,

and there is none like me,

Declaring the end from the beginning,

and from ancient times the things that are not yet done,

saying, my counsel shall stand,

and I will do all my pleasure.

Lamentations 5:19

Thou, O LORD, remainest for ever;

thy throne from generation to generation.

1 Timothy 1:17

Now unto the King eternal, immortal, invisible,

the only wise God,

be honour and glory for ever and ever. Amen.

Revelation 1:8

I am Alpha and Omega,

the beginning and the ending,

saith the Lord,

which is, and which was,

and which is to come, the Almighty.

ENGLISH STANDARD VERSION
ASSIGNMENT 1
KNOWING GOD AS ETERNAL

Job 36:26
Behold, God is great, and we know him not;

the number of his years is unsearchable.

Psalm 90:2
Before the mountains were brought forth,

or ever you had formed the earth and the world,

from everlasting to everlasting

you are God.

Isaiah 46:9, 10
Remember the former things of old;

for I am God, and there is no other;

I am God, and there is none like me,

declaring the end from the beginning

and from ancient times things not yet done,

saying, 'My counsel shall stand,

and I will accomplish all my purpose.'

Lamentations 5:19
But you, O LORD, reign forever;

your throne endures to all generations.

1 Timothy 1:17

To the King of ages, immortal, invisible,

the only God,

be honor and glory forever and ever. Amen.

Revelation 1:8

"I am the Alpha and the Omega,"

says the Lord God,

"who is and who was and who is to come,

the Almighty."

HELPS AND EXPLANATIONS

JOB 36:26

God is much, much greater than we can know. We cannot begin to figure out how old He is because He has always existed and cannot be measured by any span of time.

PSALM 90:2

God has always been God. Long before He created the great mountains, long before He created this earth and everything in it – way back there in eternity past – God has always been the same living God.

ISAIAH 46:9, 10

In these verses God is telling us some great things about Himself which He wants us to "remember":

1. The beginnings of things long past – all of history testifies to the reality of God.
2. I am God alone, He says, and there is none other.
3. I am God alone, He repeats, and there is none like Me.
4. We are told that God foretells the end from the beginning. Many of the things which He foretold have already happened.
5. From ages past, God foretells the things that have not yet happened, but which will surely come to pass.
6. God says that His will, His purpose shall stand.
7. God says He will completely fulfill all of that which He pleases to do.

LAMENTATIONS 5:19

"Generation" – the period of time from parent to child, usually considered about 33 years.

God does not change. He remains forever. Thrones fall and human governments change, but God's sovereign control of all things in the world continues without interruption from one generation to another.

1 TIMOTHY 1:17

"Immortal" – not subject to death, everlasting.

"Invisible" – refers to something real, but which cannot be seen.

The air which we breathe is real, but it cannot be seen.

Here we have a fourfold description of God, and a strong expression of praise to Him for what He is:

1. God is eternal.
2. God can never die.
3. God cannot be seen, but He is real and alive forever and ever.
4. God alone knows everything there is to know.

REVELATION 1:8

"Alpha" – the first letter of the Greek alphabet, which means that God is the beginning, the first.

"Omega" – the last letter of the Greek alphabet, which means that God is the last, in the sense that He remains forever.

It was common in those days to use the first and the last letters of the alphabet to describe the whole of anything from beginning to end. God was at the beginning of things and He will be at the close. He always has existed and He always will exist. He is absolutely eternal. He is the God Who lives now, the God Who lived from all eternity, the God Who will continue to live forever and fulfill all His purposes on earth. He is the God Who is all-mighty!

KNOWING GOD AS A PERSON

PREFACE – ASSIGNMENT 2

God is *not* just a power like electricity or an influence like kindness, but He is a real person. He is a Spirit (John 4:24), He thinks, He knows, He plans, He acts. When He wanted people to know what He was really like, He sent His Son, the Lord Jesus, into the world (John 1:14,18). Jesus said, "He that hath seen Me hath seen the Father" (John 14:9).

Because God is a real person, He desires to have fellowship with us. That is why Christ died for our sins, arose from the dead and now lives in heaven – in order that He might save, cleanse and make new all those who would receive Him (John 1:12; 2 Corinthians 5:17).

When Galileo was being tried for believing and teaching that the earth revolved around the sun, he said to his judges, "I can convince you. Look through my telescope and see for yourselves." They refused to look. They did not want to believe it. Of course, their unbelief did not change the facts; neither does the unbelief of some people change the fact that God is a person, that He loves, that Christ died for our sins, and that all who trust Him are saved.

KING JAMES VERSION
ASSIGNMENT 2
KNOWING GOD AS A PERSON

Genesis 1:27

So God created man in his own image,

in the image of God created he him;

male and female created he them.

Isaiah 42:8

I am the LORD: that is my name:

and my glory will I not give to another,

neither my praise to graven images.

Isaiah 43:11

I, even I, am the LORD;

and beside me there is no saviour.

Jeremiah 10:10

But the LORD is the true God,

he is the living God, and an everlasting king:

at his wrath the earth shall tremble,

and the nations shall not be able

to abide his indignation.

John 1:18

No man hath seen God at any time;

the only begotten Son,

which is in the bosom of the Father,

he hath declared him.

John 17:3

And this is life eternal,

that they might know thee

the only true God, and Jesus Christ,

whom thou hast sent.

1 Corinthians 8:6

But to us there is but one God, the Father,

of whom are all things, and we in him;

and one Lord Jesus Christ,

by whom are all things, and we by him.

ENGLISH STANDARD VERSION
ASSIGNMENT 2
KNOWING GOD AS A PERSON

Genesis 1:27

So God created man in his own image,

in the image of God he created him;

male and female he created them.

Isaiah 42:8

I am the LORD; that is my name;

my glory I give to no other,

nor my praise to carved idols.

Isaiah 43:11

I, I am the LORD,

and besides me there is no savior.

Jeremiah 10:10

But the LORD is the true God;

he is the living God and the everlasting King.

At his wrath the earth quakes,

and the nations cannot

endure his indignation.

John 1:18

No one has ever seen God;

the only God,

who is at the Father's side,

he has made him known.

John 17:3

And this is eternal life,

that they know you

the only true God, and Jesus Christ

whom you have sent.

1 Corinthians 8:6

Yet for us there is one God, the Father,

from whom are all things and for whom we exist,

and one Lord, Jesus Christ,

through whom are all things and through whom we exist.

HELPS AND EXPLANATIONS

Genesis 1:27

All of us know that man is a person, a real living person. This verse tells us that man was created in the "image of God," which proves that God must surely be a *real* person. Actually, God is the *greatest* Person in all the universe, and apart from Him and His power to create and sustain, there would be no other persons, no life whatsoever.

Isaiah 42:8

"Graven" – carved or formed.

God declares emphatically through the prophet Isaiah that He is a person, that He has a name, and that He will not share His rightful glory and honor with any *created* being, much less so with any dead image carved out of wood or melted into shape out of metal.

Isaiah 43:11

How precious is this short verse which tells us that there is only one God and one Savior. As the trial on Mount Carmel in Elijah's time ended with the shout of the convinced witnesses, "The LORD, he is the God: the LORD, he is the God" (1 Kings 18:39), we also exclaim with heartfelt praise, "For there is one God, and one mediator between God and men, the man Christ Jesus; who gave Himself a ransom for all …" (1 Timothy 2:5, 6).

Jeremiah 10:10

"Indignation" – anger, wrath, righteous displeasure.

In contrast to the idols, which are but imaginary gods, our wonderful God is described as being "true," "living" and "everlasting." When our God moves and acts against sin in righteous anger, the earth trembles and proud nations shrink away in great fear.

John 1:18

"Only begotten" – Christ is the One Who is most closely united to God the Father from all eternity, and Who is equal to Him in all things.

"Declared" – Christ, in His life and work, gave a full explanation of the Father.

Christ revealed God the Father as a person Who hates sin to the uttermost, but Who loves the sinners. No one has seen God at any time, but in Christ all may witness the wisdom, holiness, compassion and power of God in the fullest possible way.

John 17:3

Here we have it stated so clearly that our God is "*the only true God,*" as opposed to idols and false gods with which the heathen religions had filled the earth. We also learn that Jesus Christ came from the Father to die for our sins and "to seek and to save that which was lost." Jesus Christ is God and He came to reveal the Father. We can never have God as our heavenly Father without receiving God the Son as personal Savior. Our Lord said, "Let not your heart be troubled: ye believe in God, believe also in Me. Believe Me that I am in the Father, and the Father in Me ... (John 14:1, 11).

There is a story told about the poor man who lived in a far-away land. His only child was a small boy, and he worked for a great King in a palace close by. This King was unusual, for he had the power to make himself invisible, and only those whose eyes had been touched by the King could see him.

Every night the boy would sit on his father's knee and listen to the thrilling stories of how great, how wise, how kind and good the King was, and that someday the King would invite him to live in the beautiful palace where he would never be hungry, cold or tired any more. When the boy asked why he worked for the King, his father's reply was always the same, "Because I love him and he loves me and has done so much for me."

The more his father talked about the King, the more the boy wished to see him. One night he said to his father, "I wish I could see the King." His father replied. "Then you *shall see* him this very night." "But what about my shabby clothes?" cried the boy. His father wisely answered, "Don't you know that he would rather have you come just as you are?"

When they arrived inside the palace, it was far more beautiful than the boy had ever imagined. At one end was something that looked like a throne, but it seemed vacant. Just then the father spoke, "I have brought thee my son, oh gracious King. He wants to know you and to see you." The King quickly answered, "I am glad you have come, for I have been waiting for you. I am your friend. I have power to change your life, so put your hand in mine."

The boy put out his hand, which was firmly grasped by the strong hand of the King; immediately the boy's eyes were touched, and he saw the King in his beauty. They talked a long while, and the King told him that some day the boy would come to live with him in the palace forever.

That is just a story, but it illustrates the truth that there is a great and wonderful King who wants to be your Savior and your friend. He is the Lord Jesus Christ. He loves you. He died for your sins. *Do you know Him?* Just put your trust in Him, just reach out your hand of faith and He will grasp it and hold you forever. Your understanding will be opened to appreciate His love and to worship Him, and you will say, "I love Him because He first loved me!" "*This is life eternal*"!

1 Corinthians 8:6

God the Father is a person, "of whom are all things." He is the source of all things. "For in Him we live, and move, and have our being" (Acts 17:28). Jesus Christ, God the Son, is a person, "*by whom are all things, and we by Him.*" All things are of the Father, but they were created by the Son. That is what John 1:3 teaches. In Colossians we are told that by Christ all things were created, and that He is "before all things, and by Him all things consist" (1:16, 17). We also are "by him." It is by Christ that we are saved!

JESUS!
THE VERY THOUGHT OF THEE

Jesus! the very thought of Thee
With sweetness fills my breast;
But better far Thy face to see,
And in Thy presence rest.

No voice can sing, no heart can frame,
Nor can the memory find
A sweeter sound than Thy blest name,
O Savior of mankind!

O hope of every contrite heart,
O joy of all the meek,
To those who fall, how kind Thou art;
How good to those who seek!

But what to those who find? Ah, this
No tongue, nor pen can show;
The love of Jesus! what it is
None but His loved ones know.

Savior, our only joy be Thou,
As Thou our crown shalt be;
Be Thou, O Lord, our glory now,
And through eternity.

From the German, 17th Century

KNOWING GOD AS CREATOR

The Bible teaches that God is the Creator of all things. The very first verse in the Bible says, "In the beginning God created the heaven and the earth." If we do not accept this, we will have serious problems with the rest of the Bible. It is like the bottom block of a tall stack.

Those who refuse to believe the Bible have tried to convince us that the world came into being some other way, but they can never explain it. We thank God that we can accept the plain teaching of the Bible and just believe that our great and infinite God created all things (Hebrews 11:3).

A famous professor was trying to explain plants and flowers to a group of children. He told how plants were built up of tiny cells, and how all these cells were filled with a wonderful substance called *protoplasm*, a substance which is contained in all living bodies and which makes them live and grow. Then he said that no one knew what gave this protoplasm its power of living and growing. That was a closed door, and behind the door was just a mystery!

Then one of the children said, *"Please sir, does God live behind that closed door?"* Yes, behind every "closed door," behind every beginning is God, the eternal God, the Creator of all things.

KING JAMES VERSION

ASSIGNMENT 3

KNOWING GOD AS CREATOR

Exodus 20:11

For in six days the LORD made heaven and earth,

the sea, and all that in them is,

and rested the seventh day:

wherefore the LORD blessed the sabbath day,

and hallowed it.

Job 33:4

The Spirit of God hath made me,

and the breath of the Almighty

hath given me life.

Psalm 33:6, 7

By the word of the LORD were the heavens made;

and all the host of them

by the breath of his mouth.

He gathereth the waters of the sea together as an heap:

he layeth up the depth in storehouses.

Psalm 33:9

For he spake, and it was done;

he commanded, and it stood fast.

Jeremiah 27:5

I have made the earth,

the man and the beast

that are upon the ground,

by my great power

and by my outstretched arm,

and have given it unto whom

it seemed meet unto me.

John 1:3

All things were made by him;

and without him

was not any thing made that was made.

ENGLISH STANDARD VERSION
ASSIGNMENT 3
KNOWING GOD AS CREATOR

Exodus 20:11

For in six days the LORD made heaven and earth,

the sea, and all that is in them,

and rested on the seventh day.

Therefore the LORD blessed the Sabbath day

and made it holy.

Job 33:4

The Spirit of God has made me,

and the breath of the Almighty

gives me life.

Psalm 33:6, 7

By the word of the LORD the heavens were made,

and by the breath of his mouth all their host.

He gathers the waters of the sea as a heap;

he puts the deeps in storehouses.

Psalm 33:9

For he spoke, and it came to be;

he commanded, and it stood firm.

Jeremiah 27:5

"It is I who by my great power

and my outstretched arm

have made the earth,

with the men and animals

that are on the earth,

and I give it to whomever

it seems right to me."

John 1:3

All things were made through him,

and without him

was not any thing made that was made.

HELPS AND EXPLANATIONS

Exodus 20:11

"Hallowed" – made it sacred and different from all other days.

God created the heaven and the earth: He created all the animals; He created all living creatures in the sea; He created Adam and Eve. We learn all this in detail in the first chapters of Genesis. "In the beginning" refers to the absolute beginning of created things. You cannot go beyond this. There is nothing beyond this but God. Genesis records the beginning of time. It does not tell us *when* the "beginning" was, but it clearly states that there was a "beginning." We are told that God did all this in six days.

On the seventh day God rested and said that it should be a special day, a sacred day in which we should also rest and worship God. Following the resurrection of Christ, that special day was changed to the first day of the week,

known as the Lord's Day, in which we are to devote our
time and energies for the Lord (1 Corinthians 16:2;
Revelation 1:10).

Job 33:4

How true and how satisfying to be able to say simply and
directly that it is God Who made *me* and that it is the Almighty
God Who breathed into me the breath of life (Genesis 2:7).
There is no other explanation for the origin of life.

Psalm 33:6, 7, 9

Attention is here called to God's great power in creation,
which should move us to reverence and to worship of Him.
What He commands is *done*, and what he does *stands fast*.

God spoke this structure of the earth and the heavens
and all its glorious stars into existence, not with great pains
and time, or the help of many specialists and instruments
as men do with far lesser works, but with a single word He
commanded the universe into reality. This world, yea, this

universe and all that there is in it was called into being by the word of Almighty God.

The waters of the sea "as an heap" no doubt refers to the mighty waves of the oceans, and the "depth in storehouses" refers either to the clouds or to the springs and fountains in the heart of the earth.

Jeremiah 27:5

God declares through the prophet Jeremiah that He is the Creator of human beings, of animals and of all the creatures on land and sea. He did this by His great power as Almighty God, and as such, He is the Ruler and Sovereign over all.

John 1:3

As we are told in Ephesians 3:9, God "created all things" by Jesus Christ. Let us receive Him personally, worship Him, adore Him and serve Him, our great Lord and Savior Jesus Christ.

An unbeliever once spoke very scornfully about God taking a "piece of mud in hand, breathing on it, and changing it into a man."

There sat in the audience a saved man who could hardly stand to hear the unbeliever talk like that about God. Finally, he got up and said, "I will not discuss the creation of man with you, but I will tell you this: God stooped down and picked up the dirtiest bit of mud in our town. He breathed upon it by His Spirit and it was created anew. He changed it from a wicked wretch into a man who now hates his former sins, and who now loves the God Who saved him. I was that bit of mud."

One day, W. E. Gladstone, the great prime minister of Britain, was visiting Queen Victoria. "In all your wide reading," she said, "what in your judgment is the most sublime passage in literature?" Gladstone answered promptly with great conviction, "The first verse of the first chapter of Genesis, Your Majesty: 'In the beginning God created the heaven and the earth.' "

GOD CALLED
HIS ANCIENT PEOPLE

PREFACE – ASSIGNMENT 4

God called Abram to be the father of His people Israel. From Abraham and his wife Sarah, God raised up the nation of Israel to be His special people from whom would come the Messiah, Jesus Christ. God gave

Abraham's family many promises contained in writings called "covenants." God's covenant people Israel have been known as "Hebrews," "Israelites," and finally, as "Jews." The Jewish race has existed for about 4,000 years, and God used them to write the Scriptures and to shine the truth of the one true God to the rest of the world (Romans 3:1, 2; 9:3-5). All the non-Jewish people are called "Gentiles," or "the nations." Before the call of Abram, there were neither Jews nor Gentiles. Over thousands of years, God faithfully shepherded His people Israel to prepare the way for the coming of our Savior Jesus, who would "gather together in one the children of God" (John 11:52).

God gave Abraham's people the Promised Land of Israel as their dwelling place. God promised to make Abraham's people a great nation and God promised to bless Abraham with a permanent blessing that would eventually reach all the families of the earth (Genesis 12:1-3). Over the centuries, God blessed the Jews far beyond what they deserved and chastened them for their disobedience by removing them from their land and scattering them among the nations. But God has not forgotten the Jews, and is keeping all His covenant promises to them, including His new covenant through Jesus Christ.

KING JAMES VERSION
ASSIGNMENT 4
GOD CALLED
HIS ANCIENT PEOPLE

Genesis 12:1-3

Now the LORD had said unto Abram,

Get thee out of thy country, and from thy kindred,

and from thy father's house,

unto a land that I will shew thee:

And I will make of thee a great nation,

and I will bless thee, and make thy name great;

and thou shalt be a blessing:

And I will bless them that bless thee,

and curse him that curseth thee:

and in thee shall all families of the earth be blessed.

Genesis 17:7

And I will establish my covenant between me and thee

and thy seed after thee in their generations

for an everlasting covenant, to be a God unto thee,

and to thy seed after thee.

Deuteronomy 7:6

For thou art an holy people unto the LORD thy God:

the LORD thy God hath chosen thee

to be a special people unto himself,

above all people that are upon the face of the earth.

Psalm 89:34

My covenant will I not break,

nor alter the thing that is gone out of my lips.

Hebrews 8:10

For this is the covenant that I will make

with the house of Israel after those days, saith the Lord;

I will put my laws into their mind,

and write them in their hearts: and I will be to them a God,

and they shall be to me a people.

ENGLISH STANDARD VERSION
ASSIGNMENT 4
GOD CALLED
HIS ANCIENT PEOPLE

Genesis 12:1-3

Now the LORD said to Abram,

"Go from your country and your kindred

and your father's house

to the land that I will show you.

And I will make of you a great nation,

and I will bless you and make your name great,

so that you will be a blessing.

I will bless those who bless you,

and him who dishonors you I will curse,

and in you all the families of the earth shall be blessed."

Genesis 17:7

And I will establish my covenant between me and you

and your offspring after you throughout their generations

for an everlasting covenant, to be God to you

and to your offspring after you.

Deuteronomy 7:6

"For you are a people holy to the LORD your God.

The LORD your God has chosen you

to be a people for his treasured possession,

out of all the peoples who are on the face of the earth."

Psalm 89:34

I will not violate my covenant

or alter the word that went forth from my lips.

Hebrews 8:10

For this is the covenant that I will make

with the house of Israel after those days, declares the Lord:

I will put my laws into their minds,

and write them on their hearts, and I will be their God,

and they shall be my people.

HELPS AND EXPLANATIONS

Genesis 12:1-3

Here we have a record of the very beginning of the Jewish people. God called Abram out of the land of the Chaldees to move to a new land, which later was made known to him as the land of Palestine, with specific boundaries. Abram obeyed God, went forth by faith, and this made him acceptable in the sight of God (Genesis 15:6; Hebrews 11:8).

In calling Abram out, God made several unconditional promises to him as follows:

1. I will make of you a great nation.

2. I will bless you and make your name great.

3. I will make you and your descendants a blessing to many.

4. I will bless the nation or people that bless you.

5. I will resist the nation that resists you.

6. In you and your descendants all the peoples of the earth will be blessed.

Genesis 17:7

"Establish" – set up, settle.

"Covenant" – agreement.

Abram's name was changed to Abraham, which means "the father of many nations." God reminds Abraham of the covenant that He had made with him. He informs him further that this covenant will continue with Abraham's descendants and that it is, in fact, an everlasting covenant. God undertakes to make of Abraham's descendants a *special* people who would show to all the world that He is the only true and living God.

Deuteronomy 7:6

Here we learn that the Jewish people which began with Abraham were to be distinctive from the Gentiles in a number of respects:

1. They were to be an "holy people unto the Lord," which means that they would not go along with the practices and sins of the Gentiles.

2. They were to be a "special people" because they had a special responsibility of making the true God known.

3. They were to be "above all people" in that they had been chosen for so great a task and in that they had been so favored by the living God.

Psalm 89:34

God announces once again to David and to all the Jewish people that the thing which has gone out of His lips cannot be changed. God will never break His everlasting covenant with His earthly people Israel.

Hebrews 8:10

Here in the New Testament God reminds Israel that He has not forgotten them. We see four things:

1. God will make a future covenant with the house of Israel.

2. This renewed covenant of God will be "after those days," which apparently refers to the completion of the Church and the severe trials of the Great Tribulation (Acts 15:15-18).

3. God will impress His words upon the minds and hearts of the Jewish people.

4. The Jewish people will once again know God in a real way.

49

GOD SHOWED
HIS UNLIMITED POWER

PREFACE – ASSIGNMENT 5

The God Who created all things is the God Who controls all things in all the universe. God showed His great power many times by the miracles that are recorded both in the Old and in the New Testaments. These miracles were not just things that happened by chance, nor can they be explained as being simply the strange happenings of nature. Often God worked in ways contrary to nature in various realms, including death, disease, storms, rivers and seas. They were direct, supernatural acts of God on behalf of His people.

Probably the greatest of all the miracles was the resurrection of Christ from the dead. By this God showed His power over sin, Satan, and death, and He proved to all that He can give eternal life to anyone who will receive Christ as Savior.

KING JAMES VERSION
ASSIGNMENT 5
GOD SHOWED
HIS UNLIMITED POWER

Psalm 78:13, 14

He divided the sea,

and caused them to pass through;

and he made the waters to stand as an heap.

In the daytime also

he led them with a cloud,

and all the night with a light of fire.

Jeremiah 32:27

Behold, I am the LORD, the God of all flesh:

is there any thing too hard for me?

Matthew 11:5

The blind receive their sight,

and the lame walk,

the lepers are cleansed, and the deaf hear,

the dead are raised up,

and the poor have the gospel

preached to them.

Mark 4:39

And he arose, and rebuked the wind,

and said unto the sea, Peace, be still.

And the wind ceased,

and there was a great calm.

John 17:2

As thou hast given him power over all flesh,

that he should give eternal life

to as many as thou hast given him.

Revelation 1:18

I am he that liveth, and was dead;

and, behold, I am alive for evermore, Amen;

and have the keys of hell and of death.

ENGLISH STANDARD VERSION

ASSIGNMENT 5

GOD SHOWED
HIS UNLIMITED POWER

Psalm 78:13, 14

He divided the sea

and let them pass through it,

and made the waters stand like a heap.

In the daytime

he led them with a cloud,

and all the night with a fiery light.

Jeremiah 32:27

"Behold, I am the LORD, the God of all flesh.

Is anything too hard for me?"

Matthew 11:5

The blind receive their sight

and the lame walk,

lepers are cleansed and the deaf hear,

and the dead are raised up,

and the poor have good news

preached to them.

Mark 4:39

And he awoke and rebuked the wind

and said to the sea, "Peace! Be still!"

And the wind ceased,

and there was a great calm.

John 17:2

Since you have given him authority over all flesh,

to give eternal life

to all whom you have given him.

Revelation 1:18

And the living one. I died,

and behold I am alive forevermore,

and I have the keys of Death and Hades.

HELPS AND EXPLANATIONS

Psalm 78:13, 14

Some of the miracles of God while leading His people Israel out of Egypt and across the great sand plains are these:

1. He divided the Red Sea, made the waters to rise up into a heap, and enabled the people to pass through the sea on dry ground (Exodus 15:8).

2. In the daytime, God led the people with a cloud which provided a shade from the scorching heat and directed them in the way that they should go.

3. During the night, He overshadowed them with a blazing fire.

Jeremiah 32:27

"Flesh" – This refers especially to people.

God Himself tells us through the prophet Jeremiah that there is nothing too hard for Him. No man can ever say that.

Matthew 11:5

Only God could work the miracles that are listed in this verse. Jesus did them because He is God and His power cannot be limited, nor can it be fully understood by human beings.

Mark 4:39

"Rebuked" – checked; stopped by a strong command.

By His Word alone, Jesus commanded the wind and waves to be still. Immediately the wind stopped and everything was quiet and calm. This is Jesus our Lord! This is God! No one can ever measure His power.

John 17:2

The Lord Jesus Christ has power and authority over all mankind, even as far as being able to give people eternal life according to the will of God and their faith in Christ.

Revelation 1:18

Jesus Christ tells us that He had died, but that He arose from the dead and shall die no more. He now has power over death and over the state of the dead. Just like he who has the keys of a house can let in or shut out whom he pleases, so Christ has the full power to take to heaven or throw into hell whom He pleases. We know from Scripture that He wants to throw no one into hell and that He will surely take to heaven all those who put their trust in Him (John 5:24).

GOD WORKED THROUGH HIS INSPIRED PROPHETS

PREFACE – ASSIGNMENT 6

God worked through His inspired prophets in many different ways. Moses talked to Pharaoh on behalf of the Jewish people; then he led them out of Egypt across the Red Sea and through the wilderness. God used Elijah to warn King Ahab, and to prove to all the people that the prophets of Baal were false. Isaiah, Jeremiah and other prophets spoke the message of God to the Jewish people and warned them that they would be conquered by a heathen nation unless they really turned to God. Daniel interpreted dreams of heathen kings. Haggai, Zechariah and Malachi were used of God to encourage those who returned to Jerusalem from Babylon.

One of the most outstanding ways in which God used the prophets, including those in New Testament times, was in foretelling things that would happen hundreds and thousands of years in the future. Much of what they foretold deals with the nation Israel and with the birth, the life, death, resurrection and return of our Lord Jesus Christ. These men spoke "as they were moved by the Holy Spirit" (2 Peter 1:21), and through them God gave us His Word.

KING JAMES VERSION
ASSIGNMENT 6
GOD WORKED THROUGH HIS INSPIRED PROPHETS

Isaiah 6:8

Also I heard the voice of the Lord,

saying, Whom shall I send,

and who will go for us?

Then said I, Here am I; send me.

Jeremiah 30:2

Thus speaketh the LORD God of Israel,

saying, Write thee all the words

that I have spoken unto thee in a book.

Haggai 1:13

Then spake Haggai the LORD's messenger

in the LORD's message unto the people,

saying, I am with you, saith the LORD.

Zechariah 4:6

Then he answered and spake unto me,

saying, This is the word of the LORD

unto Zerubbabel, saying,

Not by might, nor by power,

but by my spirit, saith the LORD of hosts.

Luke 24:27

And beginning at Moses and all the prophets,

he expounded unto them in all the scriptures

the things concerning himself.

James 5:17, 18

Elias was a man subject to like passions as we are,

and he prayed earnestly that it might not rain:

and it rained not on the earth

by the space of three years and six months.

And he prayed again, and the heaven gave rain,

and the earth brought forth her fruit.

ENGLISH STANDARD VERSION

ASSIGNMENT 6

GOD WORKED THROUGH HIS INSPIRED PROPHETS

Isaiah 6:8

And I heard the voice of the LORD

saying, "Whom shall I send,

and who will go for us?"

Then I said, "Here am I! Send me."

Jeremiah 30:2

"Thus says the LORD, the God of Israel:

Write in a book

all the words that I have spoken to you."

Haggai 1:13

Then Haggai, the messenger of the LORD,

spoke to the people with the LORD'S message,

"I am with you, declares the LORD."

Zechariah 4:6

Then he said to me,

"This is the word of the LORD

to Zerubbabel:

Not by might, nor by power,

but by my Spirit, says the LORD of hosts."

Luke 24:27

And beginning with Moses and all the Prophets,

he interpreted to them in all the Scriptures

the things concerning himself.

James 5:17, 18

Elijah was a man with a nature like ours,

and he prayed fervently that it might not rain,

and for three years and six months

it did not rain on the earth.

Then he prayed again, and heaven gave rain,

and the earth bore its fruit.

HELPS AND EXPLANATIONS

Isaiah 6:8

The prophet Isaiah "saw" the LORD in His holiness, he saw himself and his people in their sinfulness, he was cleansed, and then he "heard the voice of the LORD." He responded quickly in saying not only that he was *willing* to go forth in the service of God, but he stated specifically, "*Here am I: send me*" (Isaiah 6:1-8).

Jeremiah 30:2

It is good to note that the "word that came to Jeremiah" was "from the LORD" (Jeremiah 30:1). God asked the prophet to write all the words He had spoken to him "in a book." This is how God used the prophets in giving us the Bible (2 Peter 1:21).

Haggai 1:13

"Haggai" – the name of the prophet.

This is an example of how God used the prophet Haggai called "the LORD's messenger" to speak "the LORD's message" to the Lord's people when they were doing the Lord's work in rebuilding the temple in the days of Zerubbabel and Ezra. How encouraging is "the LORD's message": "*I am with you, saith the LORD.*"

Zechariah 4:6

"Zechariah" – the name of the prophet.

"Zerubbabel" – The name of the man whom God used to lead the small group of Jewish people from Babylon to Jerusalem in order to rebuild the temple. This is recorded in the book of Ezra.

We have here another example of instruction from the Lord to the group of Jews that returned to Jerusalem from Babylon in order to rebuild the temple. Zerubbabel was their leader, and God spoke to him and the people through the prophet Zechariah; God reminded them that their task was great, and that it would be done through the power of God's Spirit and not simply through their own methods and might.

Luke 24:27

"Expounded" – explained in detail.

This is most significant! You see, the Lord Jesus Christ knew and believed the Old Testament Scriptures. He knew clearly the many passages where the prophets spoke concerning Him; and the record says, "beginning with Moses" and then "all the prophets." He taught them from those Scriptures the truths concerning Himself.

James 5:17, 18

"Passions" – nature, emotions. Elijah was a man with a nature like ours.

We are taught here that a prophet like Elijah, though very great, was but a human being like one of us. We are taught that he was fully dependent upon God just as we are and that he prayed "earnestly." He prayed that it would not rain for three and a half years, and then he prayed that it *would* rain. God answered his prayers. This is a fuller revelation of what we find in 1 Kings 17 and 18.

THE GOD OF INFINITE LOVE

PREFACE – ASSIGNMENT 7

God's love has no limits. It cannot be measured. Love is so much a part of God that the Apostle John wrote, "God is love" (1 John 4:8).

Although it is impossible ever fully to understand the love of God, He wants us to meditate upon it and to find out all we can about it. It is something like the study of the ocean, or like flights into space. There will always be more beyond what we discover, but all that we find out thrills us and makes us want to learn more. The more we find out about God's infinite love, the more we love Him.

We have the greatest display of the love of God in the coming of the Lord Jesus Christ into the world to die for our sins. God so loved the world that He gave His only Son to take upon Himself our sins and the sins of the whole world, and to suffer untold agony upon the cruel cross in our stead.

"Oh, love of God, how rich and pure!

How measureless and strong!

It shall forever more endure –

The saints' and angels' song."

F. M. Lehman

KING JAMES VERSION
ASSIGNMENT 7
THE GOD OF INFINITE LOVE

Jeremiah 31:3

The LORD hath appeared of old unto me,

saying, Yea, I have loved thee

with an everlasting love:

therefore with lovingkindness have I drawn thee.

John 17:23

I in them, and thou in me,

that they may be made perfect in one;

and that the world may know

that thou hast sent me,

and hast loved them, as thou hast loved me.

Ephesians 3:17-19

That Christ may dwell in your hearts by faith;

that ye, being rooted and grounded in love,

May be able to comprehend with all saints

what is the breadth, and length,

and depth, and height;

And to know the love of Christ,

which passeth knowledge,

that ye might be filled with all the fulness of God.

1 John 3:1

Behold, what manner of love

the Father hath bestowed upon us,

that we should be called the sons of God:

therefore the world knoweth us not,

because it knew him not.

1 John 4:9

In this was manifested

the love of God toward us,

because that God sent

his only begotten Son into the world,

that we might live through him.

ENGLISH STANDARD VERSION
ASSIGNMENT 7
THE GOD OF INFINITE LOVE

Jeremiah 31:3
The LORD appeared to him from far away.
I have loved you
with an everlasting love;
therefore I have continued my faithfulness to you.

John 17:23
I in them and you in me,
that they may become perfectly one,
so that the world may know
that you sent me
and loved them even as you loved me.

Ephesians 3:17-19
So that Christ may dwell in your hearts through faith –
that you, being rooted and grounded in love,
may have strength to comprehend with all the saints

what is the breadth and length
and height and depth,

and to know the love of Christ
that surpasses knowledge,
that you may be filled with all the fullness of God.

1 John 3:1

See what kind of love

the Father has given to us,

that we should be called children of God; and so we are.

The reason why the world does not know us

is that it did not know him.

1 John 4:9

In this the love of God

was made manifest among us,

that God sent

his only Son into the world,

so that we might live through him.

HELPS AND EXPLANATIONS

Jeremiah 31:3

Although in a primary sense, this verse applies to the Jewish nation, yet it is for us also. God's love is not a temporary love shown to one generation, but rather, it is an *everlasting* love. Is it not also true that in the experience of each one of us who is saved, God may well say, "With lovingkindness have I drawn thee."? God is so patient with sinners; He surrounds them with the riches of His goodness in order that they might repent and turn to Him (Romans 2:4).

John 17:23

Our Lord is speaking to the Father about the real and complete unity that exists between them – God the Father and God the Son; then He prays that all believers on the earth might experience such real unity in order that the world may be convinced that Christ is, indeed, the Messiah sent down from heaven.

That last statement in the verse is most significant for this assignment: Thou *"hast loved them, as thou hast loved me."* God loves us just as much as He loves Christ. This is truly *infinite* love. We cannot think of any greater, deeper, or more enduring love than that.

Ephesians 3:17-19

"Grounded" – founded, settled down.

"Comprehend" – understand fully; grasp firmly.

The Apostle Paul is praying for the believers:

1. That Christ may be *enthroned* in their hearts. Christ dwelling in the heart of the believer here suggests the idea of Christ reigning and controlling that life.

2. That believers may be fully *established* – "rooted and grounded in love." *Rooted* like a tree in the ground, and *grounded* like a building which is built upon a solid foundation. But rooted and grounded in what? "*In love!*" That is the great rock foundation upon which we build – the love of God and the God of love.

3. That believers might be *enlightened* in grasping more fully the greatness of the love of Christ "with all saints." None of us will ever be able to take it all in, but if you take in a little, another Christian a little, and if I comprehend a little, then together, "with all saints" we can begin to get some idea of the love of Christ.

The Apostle speaks about "the breadth, and length, and depth and height" of the love of Christ. We all know the *three* dimensions – length, width and thickness, but what is that fourth dimension? How would you draw a picture of it? Perhaps we could call it a *spiritual* dimension.

The skeleton of a Spanish prisoner was once found in a dungeon. The body and the clothing were all gone, but a chain was still attached to the ankle bone. Close beside, upon the wall, they saw cut into the rock, probably with a sharp piece of metal, a cross. Above the cross, carved in Spanish letters, was the word for "height," below it, the word for "depth," on the one arm the word for "length" and on the other arm, the word for "breadth." As the poor prisoner was starving to death, he was thinking about the wonder of the love of Christ "which passeth knowledge." To him the figure of Christ dying for us on the cross summed it all up – the breadth, the length, the depth, the height. Such love for poor unworthy sinners is too great for us to understand. It passes the limits and powers of our ability to know.

4. That believers might be *enriched* as they are "filled with all the fulness of God." Indeed, even the "heaven of heavens cannot contain" all the fullness of God, but like the seashell on the shore is filled with all the fullness of the ocean when the tide comes rolling in, so we may be filled and enriched with His fullness, while the great vastness of it is infinitely beyond our ability to hold or to grasp.

1 John 3:1

"Bestowed" – gave.

"*What manner of love.*" This speaks about the *kind* of love and the degree or extent of that love. God adopts believers into His family, allowing them to call Him their heavenly Father, and so the *kind* of God's love is most tender and most precious. God has drawn vile, rebellious sinners to Himself, made them into new creations, clothed them with the righteousness of Christ, and so in *degree*, the love of God is the highest and the greatest.

A king could show no greater love for a wandering, ragged, sinful orphan boy found in the streets than by adopting him into his own family, and admitting him to the same privileges and honors as his own sons. Yet, this would be but a little thing compared with the honor which God has bestowed upon us in His great love "that we should be called the sons of God."

1 John 4:9

"Manifested" – shown, made clear.

The most outstanding way in which God's love has been shown for us and proved to us is in the fact that God sent His only Son into the world to die for our sins, so that by receiving Him, we might have life eternal.

THE SAVIOR'S LOVE

See, oh see, what love the Savior
Also hath on us bestowed;
How He bled for us and suffered,
How He bare the heavy load.
On the cross and in the garden
Oh how sore was His distress!
Is not this a love that passeth
Aught that tongue can e'er express?

Frances Ridley Havergal

HIS LOVE UNSPEAKABLE

And then I thought of Him Who fed
Five thousand hungry men,
With five small casual loaves of bread,
Would He were here again!
Dear God! hast Thou still miracles
For the troubled sons of men?

He has, He will, He worketh still,
In ways most wonderful.
He drew me from the miry clay,
He filled my cup quite full,
And while my heart can speak I'll tell
His love unspeakable.

John Oxenham

THE GOD OF AMAZING GRACE

PREFACE – ASSIGNMENT 8

The word *grace* means kindness and favor that is not earned or deserved. Yet it is much more than that – it is a kindness shown to someone who fully deserves justice and punishment. If God gave us what we deserved, we would all be condemned to eternal punishment because of our sin against Him. But our Lord Jesus Christ died for us and paid the full price of our sin in the sight of God. Through simple faith in Christ, the guilty sinners can be fully justified and clothed with God's perfect righteousness. In grace God pours out blessings upon the believers all their lives, and then He takes them to heaven.

During the Civil War a prisoner was pardoned by President Lincoln. The man who had been so full of bitterness and rage suddenly quieted down and said, "What! Has Abraham Lincoln pardoned me? Why?" The officer who brought the pardon said, "If you got *what you deserved* you would be shot, but someone interceded for you in Washington and obtained your pardon; you have liberty if you will accept it."

The man instantly received it, and was so broken up by this expression of undeserved kindness that it led to his conversion soon after.

KING JAMES VERSION
ASSIGNMENT 8
THE GOD OF AMAZING GRACE

Exodus 34:6

And the LORD passed by before him,

and proclaimed, The LORD, The LORD God,

merciful and gracious, longsuffering,

and abundant in goodness and truth.

Psalm 86:15

But thou, O Lord, art a God full of compassion,

and gracious, longsuffering,

and plenteous in mercy and truth.

Micah 7:18

Who is a God like unto thee,

that pardoneth iniquity,

and passeth by the transgression

of the remnant of his heritage?

he retaineth not his anger for ever,

because he delighteth in mercy.

2 Corinthians 8:9

For ye know the grace of our Lord Jesus Christ,

that, though he was rich,

yet for your sakes he became poor,

that ye through his poverty might be rich.

1 Timothy 1:14

And the grace of our Lord

was exceeding abundant with faith and love

which is in Christ Jesus.

Titus 3:7

That being justified by his grace,

we should be made heirs

according to the hope of eternal life.

1 Peter 5:10

But the God of all grace,

who hath called us unto his eternal glory

by Christ Jesus,

after that ye have suffered a while,

make you perfect, stablish, strengthen, settle you.

ASSIGNMENT 8

THE GOD OF AMAZING GRACE

Exodus 34:6

The LORD passed before him

and proclaimed, "The LORD, the LORD,

a God merciful and gracious, slow to anger,

and abounding in steadfast love and faithfulness."

Psalm 86:15

But you, O Lord, are a God merciful and gracious,

slow to anger

and abounding in steadfast love and faithfulness.

Micah 7:18

Who is a God like you,

pardoning iniquity

and passing over transgression

for the remnant of his inheritance?

He does not retain his anger forever,

because he delights in steadfast love.

2 Corinthians 8:9

For you know the grace of our Lord Jesus Christ,

that though he was rich,

yet for your sake he became poor,

so that you by his poverty might become rich.

1 Timothy 1:14

And the grace of our Lord

overflowed for me with the faith and love

that are in Christ Jesus.

Titus 3:7

So that being justified by his grace

we might become heirs

according to the hope of eternal life.

1 Peter 5:10

And after you have suffered a little while,

the God of all grace, who has called you

to his eternal glory in Christ,

will himself restore,

confirm, strengthen, and establish you.

HELPS AND EXPLANATIONS

Exodus 34:6

The Lord God is "merciful" means that He is deeply compassionate.

The Lord God is "gracious" means that He shows favor to those who deserve punishment.

The Lord God is "longsuffering" means that He holds back His anger.

The Lord God is "abundant in goodness and truth," means that He delights to show lovingkindness, and that He is steadfast and faithful in it.

Psalm 86:15

This verse is very similar to Exodus 34:6. Our God is a "God full of compassion" for lost and sinful humanity. He has proved it by giving His only Son as a sacrifice for our sins and by showering us with good gifts and benefits day by day. "He that spared not his own Son, but delivered him up for us all, how shall he not with him also freely give us all things?" (Romans 8:32).

Micah 7:18

"Iniquity" – sin, evil.

"Transgression" – sin against lawful authority.

"Remnant" – survivors; those who are left.

"Heritage" – inheritance; God's own people were His inheritance.

"Retaineth" – holds, keeps.

Our God is so wonderful because He "delighteth in mercy." He is just, but Scripture does not say that He *delights* in giving out that which people justly deserve. It says He enjoys showing mercy because He "is rich in mercy, for His great love wherewith He loved us" (Ephesians 2:4). Therefore, He pardons iniquity, He forgives rebellion and although He hates sin, He does not dwell on His anger, but He ever works and moves to show mercy.

2 Corinthians 8:9

Here is the grace of our Lord Jesus Christ that expressed itself so freely to those who deserved something else. Though "He was rich" – the heir of heaven, the Lord of all creation, filled with all the fullness of the Godhead yet for our sakes "He became poor." He stripped Himself of His robes of glory, and clothed Himself with a human body with all of its weaknesses and limitations. Then He became obedient unto death, even the death on the cross, which was usually reserved for the worst of criminals (Philippians 2:6-8).

Jesus gave everything:

He gave His head to the crown of thorns.

He gave His back to the cruel lash.

He gave His cheeks to those who plucked out the hairs.

He gave His face to dirty human spittle.

He gave His shoulders to be draped with the robe of mockers.

He gave His clothes to His murderers.

He gave His hands and feet to be nailed to the accursed cross.

He gave His blood for the remission of sins.

He gave His body as an offering for sin.

He gave His spirit to God after that He had suffered alone.

"That ye through His poverty might be rich." What a glorious exchange! He became poor that we might become rich. He took upon Himself our sins so that we might receive the righteousness of God through faith (2 Corinthians 5:21). He endured the anguish of hell that we might enjoy the blessings of heaven.

1 Timothy 1:14

The grace of our Lord Jesus Christ was more than abundant. It inspires faith and love which centers in Christ.

The grace of our Lord Jesus Christ may be feebly illustrated by a story about a sergeant who told how he was saved while he was in the army.

"We had a private in our company who lived his Christianity all the time," he said. "We gave that fellow an awful time. One night we came in after having marched in a terrible rain. All of us were very wet and tired. Our one thought was to find the quickest way to get to bed. But this Christian private took time to kneel down and have his prayer time with the Lord. "This made me so angry that I picked up one of my muddy boots and threw it at him. It hit him on the side of the head, but this did not stop him from praying. I picked up my other boot and heaved it in his direction. I hit him again, but he continued to pray.

"The next morning beside my bunk stood my boots, beautifully cleaned and polished. That broke me and I was saved that day. After what I had done to him, he had shown this kindness to me."

Titus 3:7

"Justified" – made righteous in the sight of God.

Through the free love and mercy of God, a believer in Christ has the guilt of his sins forever removed, and the righteousness of Christ bestowed upon him. From that moment on, God no longer looks upon such a person in his sin, but in His Son. Believers become "heirs" to eternal life.

1 Peter 5:10

"*The God of all grace!*" What a thrilling description of God, and what an amazing definition of grace! God is the author and the giver of all grace. From Him the believer in Christ receives eternal life and the sure hope of eternal glory in heaven.

In this life, the Christian is called upon to suffer "a while," but through that suffering, God causes him to grow in grace and to become a more fruitful witness for Him.

"Make you perfect" means to make a believer more mature spiritually.

"Stablish" means to make steadfast.

"Strengthen" means to enable the Christian to stand amidst difficulties.

"Settle" means to ground firmly as upon a foundation.

FAIREST LORD JESUS

Fairest Lord Jesus,

King of creation;

O Thou of God and man the Son!

Truly I'll love Thee,

Truly I'll serve Thee,

Light of my soul, my Joy, my Crown.

Fair are the meadows,

Fairer the woodlands

Robed in the blooming garb of spring;

Jesus is fairer,

Jesus is purer,

He makes our sorrowing spirits sing.

Fair is the sunshine,

Fairer the moonlight,

And all the twinkling starry hosts;

Jesus shines brighter,

Jesus shines purer,

Than all the angels heaven can boast.

Silesian Folk Song

THE GOD OF UNCHANGING TRUTH

PREFACE – ASSIGNMENT 9

The ideas and writings of men are continually changing. Books on science, medicine and other subjects have to be updated every few years. New discoveries and new studies make it quite clear that what was thought to be true a few years ago can no longer be accepted as truth. In a few more years, the ideas which people in the world regard as being true today will once again become but old-fashioned theories, and new ones will take their place. This is what goes on year after year with the thoughts and writings of men.

But God's Word stands forever. "For ever, O LORD, thy word is settled in heaven" (Psalm 119:89)! It is just as true and just as up-to-date today as it was thousands of years ago when it was first written. God does not change. All truth begins with God. God makes no mistakes. He never has to apologize for any errors. God knows the end from the beginning, and what He says will always be true because He is the God of unchanging truth.

KING JAMES VERSION

ASSIGNMENT 9

THE GOD OF UNCHANGING TRUTH

Numbers 23:19

God is not a man, that he should lie;

neither the son of man,

that he should repent:

hath he said, and shall he not do it?

or hath he spoken,

and shall he not make it good?

Deuteronomy 32:4

He is the Rock, his work is perfect:

for all his ways are judgment:

a God of truth and without iniquity,

just and right is he.

Psalm 111: 7, 8

The works of his hands

are verity and judgment;

all his commandments are sure.

They stand fast for ever and ever,

and are done in truth and uprightness.

Proverbs 19:21

There are many devices in a man's heart;

nevertheless the counsel of the LORD,

that shall stand.

Hebrews 6:17, 18

Wherein God,

willing more abundantly

to shew unto the heirs of promise

the immutability of his counsel,

confirmed it by an oath:

That by two immutable things,

in which it was impossible for God to lie,

we might have a strong consolation,

who have fled for refuge

to lay hold upon the hope set before us.

ENGLISH STANDARD VERSION
ASSIGNMENT 9
THE GOD OF UNCHANGING TRUTH

Numbers 23:19

God is not man, that he should lie,

or a son of man, that he should change his mind.

Has he said, and will he not do it?

Or has he spoken,

and will he not fulfill it?

Deuteronomy 32:4

The Rock, his work is perfect;

for all his ways are justice.

A God of faithfulness and without iniquity,

just and upright is he.

Psalm 111:7, 8

The works of his hands

are faithful and just;

all his precepts are trustworthy;

they are established forever and ever,

to be performed with faithfulness and uprightness.

Proverbs 19:21

Many are the plans in the mind of a man,

but it is the purpose of the LORD

that will stand.

Hebrews 6:17, 18

So when God

desired to show more convincingly

to the heirs of the promise

the unchangeable character of his purpose,

he guaranteed it with an oath,

so that by two unchangeable things,

in which it is impossible for God to lie,

we who have fled for refuge

might have strong encouragement

to hold fast to the hope set before us.

HELPS AND EXPLANATIONS

Numbers 23:19

God never tells lies. He always speaks what is true altogether. God is not like people who often speak and promise things which they never intend to do, or cannot do, or will not do. God will always do what He promises to do (1 Thessalonians 5:24).

Deuteronomy 32:4

The word "Rock" suggests the strength and stability of God's nature. Therefore, all "His work is perfect." All His actions are right. In all His dealings with men, he is never unjust or unfair. He is a "God of truth" and without any trace of evil. His character is absolutely reliable, and He is faithful to all His promises.

Psalm 111:7, 8

"Verity" – that which is true.

All that God does is always consistent with His character and in full agreement with His Word. His promises and His commandments do not change. They are established upon the sure foundations of truth and right.

Proverbs 19:21

"Devices" – ideas, plans.

Men have various ideas and plans, many of which never come to pass. The purposes and plans of God always come to pass because they are eternal and unchangeable.

Hebrews 6: 17, 18

"Immutability" – not subject to change.

"Confirmed" – A legal term which means that God came in with a guarantee.

"Consolation" – encouragement.

"Oath" – a solemn statement in telling the truth.

Since it was God's desire to show more convincingly to the believers how unchangeable His promise really was, He guaranteed it with an oath. So that by these two unchangeable facts (the *Promise* of God and the *Oath* of God) in which it is impossible for God to be false, we believers may have a mighty encouragement to lay hold of the hope set before us.

This is a tremendous statement concerning the never-changing character of God and the never-changing nature of His promises.

GOD ESTABLISHED THE HOME

PREFACE – ASSIGNMENT 10

The Lord has given the basic pattern for the home in His Word; each member plays his or her role for God's glory, blending their roles in a God-pleasing harmony, like the high and low notes of male and female voices in a song. The husband is the head of the wife and the final authority for family decisions in the context of loving mutual submission and Christ-like love for his wife (Ephesians 5:21-25). The husband also raises his children in the training and admonition of the Lord (Ephesians 6:4). Wives submit to their husbands as to the Lord (Ephesians 5:22), and by their loving care of the household and its members, maintain a good witness of God's Word to the world (Titus 2:3-5). Both husbands and wives can contribute to the home's physical and financial needs (1 Thessalonians 2:7,11; Proverbs 31:10-31; Acts 16:14). Children are to obey their parents, listening to their instruction, responding to the correction of their parents and honoring them all the days of their lives (Ephesians 6:1-3).

KING JAMES VERSION
ASSIGNMENT 10
GOD ESTABLISHED THE HOME

Genesis 2:18, 24

And the LORD God said,

It is not good that the man should be alone;

I will make him an help meet for him.

Therefore shall a man leave his father and his mother,

and shall cleave unto his wife:

and they shall be one flesh.

Exodus 20:12

Honour thy father and thy mother:

that thy days may be long upon the land

which the LORD thy God giveth thee.

Deuteronomy 6:6, 7

And these words, which I command thee this day,

shall be in thine heart:

And thou shalt teach them diligently unto thy children,

and shalt talk of them

when thou sittest in thine house,

and when thou walkest by the way,

and when thou liest down, and when thou risest up.

Colossians 3:18-20

Wives, submit yourselves unto your own husbands,

as it is fit in the Lord.

Husbands, love your wives,

and be not bitter against them.

Children, obey your parents in all things:

for this is well pleasing unto the Lord.

ENGLISH STANDARD VERSION

ASSIGNMENT 10

GOD ESTABLISHED THE HOME

Genesis 2: 18, 24

Then the LORD God said,

"It is not good that the man should be alone;

I will make him a helper fit for him."

Therefore a man shall leave his father and his mother

and hold fast to his wife,

and they shall become one flesh.

Exodus 20:12

"Honor your father and your mother,

that your days may be long in the land

that the LORD your God is giving you."

Deuteronomy 6: 6, 7

And these words that I command you today

shall be on your heart.

You shall teach them diligently to your children,

and shall talk of them

when you sit in your house,

and when you walk by the way,

and when you lie down, and when you rise.

Colossians 3:18-20

Wives, submit to your husbands,

as is fitting in the Lord.

Husbands, love your wives,

and do not be harsh with them.

Children, obey your parents in everything,

for this pleases the Lord.

HELPS AND EXPLANATIONS

Genesis 2:18, 24

"Cleave" – cling.

God created man and then He created the woman to be a helper suited for him, because it was not good that the man should be alone.

God planned and ordered marriage between a man and a woman. Therefore, when a man and woman love one another and are brought together in a marriage union, they are to leave their parents and become united to each other so closely that they are regarded as being one person.

Exodus 20:12

Children are instructed to "honor" their father and mother. They are not only to reverence, love and obey their parents, but they are also to help them and support them as may be needed (Matthew 15:4-6). The days and years of such devoted children are prolonged by the special providence of God.

Deuteronomy 6: 6, 7

"Diligently" – earnestly and carefully.

"*These words ... shall be in thine heart.*" Whatever is in the heart comes out through the lips and through the activities of life. How important it is, then, to have the heart filled with the Word of God – so full that we will have no room for the vanities and follies of this present evil world. "For out of the abundance of the heart the mouth speaketh" (Matthew 12:34).

This is a command of God to parents, to pastors and teachers and to all who would help others spiritually – take time to store up in your heart the precious Word of God.

"*Thou shalt teach them diligently unto thy children ...*" is a command not only to parents, but to all who would be God's faithful witnesses, whether they be young or older. God's Word must be taught to the children with the greatest care, not only to help them understand the Word of God, but also that they might develop a real love and desire for God's Word. The words, "teach diligently," suggest the idea of whetting their appetite for it, as one who whets a blunt instrument again and again in order to sharpen it. Sharpening the young person's taste for the things of God requires much patience and much persistence, day and night, both at home and while away from home.

The whole idea of providing helpful rewards for memorizing Scripture and surrounding the children and young people with interesting Christian literature, plaques and games, etc. was strongly suggested by these verses when we first started.

Colossians 3:18-20

Here are God's instructions for a happy Christian home.

Wives are instructed not to be bossy, but rather, to submit themselves unto their own husbands with reverence because this is the order established by God.

Husbands are instructed to love their wives, and to set aside all back-biting and bitterness which adverse circumstances or misunderstandings may create.

Children are instructed to obey their parents in all things, not because it is easy, but because it is *right* (Ephesians 6:1), and because "this is well pleasing unto the Lord." What a thrill and joy it is to the parents when children obey their instructions and submit to their corrections.

HAPPY THE HOME

Happy the home when God is there,
And love fills every breast;
When one their wish, and one their prayer,
And one their heavenly rest.

Happy the home where Jesus' name
Is sweet to every ear;
Where children early lisp His fame,
And parents hold Him dear.

Happy the home where prayer is heard,
And praise is wont to rise;
Where parents love the Sacred Word,
And live but for the skies.

Lord, let us in our homes agree
This blest home to gain;
Unite our hearts in love to thee,
And love to all will reign.

GOD ESTABLISHED THE CHURCH

PREFACE – ASSIGNMENT 11

It is God Himself Who established the Church. According to the New Testament, the Church is not just a building or an organization. Instead, the true, complete Church is an *organism*, made up of true believers in Christ, who by the Holy Spirit are baptized into the Body of Christ. Our Lord Jesus Christ is the real Head of the Church.

The Church does indeed have buildings and often organization, but the complete Church of God goes beyond that. It is a new and unique creation of God which includes the risen Christ as Head, as well as all true believers between Pentecost and the coming of Christ for the Church.

Since all Christians are part of the Church, God has instructed them to come together for worship, prayer, fellowship and instruction. This is God's plan and not just something that people want to promote. A Christian misses much of God's blessing in his life when he fails to be a part of some good Bible-believing local church (Hebrews 10:25).

KING JAMES VERSION

ASSIGNMENT 11

GOD ESTABLISHED
THE CHURCH

Matthew 16:18

And I say also unto thee, That thou art Peter,

and upon this rock I will build my church;

and the gates of hell shall not prevail against it.

Matthew 18:20

For where two or three

are gathered together in my name,

there am I in the midst of them.

1 Corinthians 3:16

Know ye not that ye are the temple of God,

and that the Spirit of God dwelleth in you?

1 Corinthians 12:13

For by one Spirit are we all baptized into one body,

whether we be Jews or Gentiles,

whether we be bond or free;

and have been all made to drink

into one Spirit.

Ephesians 2:19, 20

Now therefore

ye are no more strangers and foreigners,

but fellow citizens with the saints,

and of the household of God;

And are built upon the foundation

of the apostles and prophets,

Jesus Christ himself

being the chief corner stone.

Colossians 1:18

And he is the head of the body, the church:

who is the beginning,

the firstborn from the dead;

that in all things

he might have the preeminence.

ENGLISH STANDARD VERSION
ASSIGNMENT 11
GOD ESTABLISHED
THE CHURCH

Matthew 16:18

"And I tell you, you are Peter,

and on this rock I will build my church,

and the gates of hell shall not prevail against it."

Matthew 18:20

"For where two or three

are gathered in my name,

there am I among them."

1 Corinthians 3:16

Do you not know that you are God's temple

and that God's Spirit dwells in you?

1 Corinthians 12:13

For in one Spirit we were all baptized into one body –

Jews or Greeks,

slaves or free –

and all were made to drink

of one Spirit.

Ephesians 2:19, 20

So then

you are no longer strangers and aliens,

But you are fellow citizens with the saints

and members of the household of God,

built on the foundation

of the apostles and prophets,

Christ Jesus himself

being the cornerstone.

Colossians 1:18

And he is the head of the body, the church.

He is the beginning,

the firstborn from the dead,

that in everything

he might be preeminent.

HELPS AND EXPLANATIONS

Matthew 16:18

"Prevail" – succeed, overcome.

The Church is never mentioned in the Old Testament. Our Lord speaks of it here for the first time; notice that He speaks of it as something that was still in the future, "I *will* build my church."

"*And upon this rock,*" Greek *petra* – very emphatic as though Christ were pointing to Himself. He is, but only in a metaphorical way. Petra is feminine gender and therefore could not refer directly to Christ nor to Peter. It must therefore refer to Peter's response in verse 16. Such a response is

covered by the Greek word *homologia*, feminine gender, and is translated *confession* in 1 Timothy 6:13 and *profession* in 1 Timothy 6:12; Hebrews 3:1, 4:14 and 10:23.

Peter, Greek *petros*, little rock, moveable and hardly capable of being a foundation for the church. Peter was neither the builder nor the foundation. Christ alone, whom Peter confessed, is the builder and the foundation. To this agrees Paul's word to the Corinthians, "For other foundation can no man lay than that is laid, which is Jesus Christ" (1 Corinthians 3:11). Peter, little rock, would hardly consider himself as the foundation. In this same context Christ rebuked him. "Get thee behind me, Satan: thou art an offence to me." (Matthew 16:23).

Furthermore, Peter himself declares that it is Jesus Christ who is the "chief corner stone" of the Church (1 Peter 2:5-6).

Matthew 18:20

The simplest form of a local assembly, which most people call a church, is made up when two or three people are gathered in His name. When they come together in His name to worship, to pray and to study His Word, He Himself is in the midst of them. It is our Lord's presence that makes such a group of people distinct.

A certain pastor tells an interesting story about the Lord's presence in a meeting:

One Sunday, I was out preaching and at the place where I took tea, I met a little boy about five or six years old. I said, "Were you at prayer meeting this morning?" "Yes," was the reply. I asked the little fellow if he could tell me how many were present. "I'll call them over, and you count," he said. I did so until I had counted seven. "Then there were seven at the prayer meeting this morning?" "Oh, no," he exclaimed, "there were eight." "You must certainly have made a mistake, my little man." He burst out in a joyous strain. "There were eight there, for the Lord was there!"

1 Corinthians 3:16

"Ye are the temple of God." The word "ye" is plural. The Spirit of God not only indwells the individual believers, but the group of *believers together* forms a sacred shrine for the Spirit of God.

1 Corinthians 12:13

We see here that it is the baptism of the Holy Spirit which places every true believer into the Body of Christ, which is the Church. This began at Pentecost (Acts 2). Since that day, whenever a sinner, whether Jew or Gentile, trusts Christ, he is at once joined to the Body of Christ, the Church, by the Spirit's baptism.

Ephesians 2:19, 20

The materials out of which the Church is constructed are the individual believers in Christ during this age, whether they be young or old, whether they be Jew or Gentile.

Before the time when the Church was begun, Gentiles were total outsiders and regarded as "strangers and foreigners," but now all believers together form "the household of God."

Notice that the "apostles and prophets" are in the "foundation," but it is Jesus Christ Himself Who is "the chief corner stone."

Colossians 1:18

"Pre-eminence" – the highest place.

The complete Church is spoken of in the Scriptures as being the Body of Christ. Let us not fail to notice the clear teaching in this verse that it is Christ Himself Who is the Head of the Church. The life and function of each member of the Church does not come as a result of his connection with the Body, but because of his direct connection with the Head. That's why it is so important for each believer to *abide* in Christ in the most personal way, from day to day, in order that he may produce fruit (John 15:1-8).

Christ is "the beginning", that is, He is the beginning of all living things. Life from nothing began through Him. Christ is "the firstborn from the dead," which means that life from the dead began through Him. He was not the first one to be raised from the dead, but He was the first one to be raised from the dead and remain alive forevermore. He is called the "first fruits of them that slept" (1 Corinthians 15:20). All the members of His Body, the Church, shall also be raised because they are permanently united to the *living* Head.

This is why Christ is worthy of the highest place in the Church, in our individual lives, yea, "in all things."

GOD ESTABLISHED HUMAN GOVERNMENT

PREFACE – ASSIGNMENT 12

Before the great flood, men became very wicked, and the thoughts of their hearts were "only evil continually" (Genesis 6:5). There were no civil authorities and everyone did as he pleased. Things became so corrupt and violent that God decided to destroy the wickedness in the earth by means of the great flood.

After the flood, when Noah and his family came out of the ark, God Himself established human government. He gave the human governors the authority to take people's lives if they disobeyed God's commandment (Genesis 9:6). All other powers of government are implied in these instructions, and these are progressively spelled out in detail in other portions of the Scriptures.

No human government is perfect. In some countries, the government is very oppressive. We must always remember that it is only sinful men who are governing other sinful men, but that *any* government is better than no government at all. God planned that governments should have power to control men, for the punishment of evil-doers and for the protection of those who try to keep the law.

KING JAMES VERSION
ASSIGNMENT 12

GOD ESTABLISHED HUMAN GOVERNMENT

Genesis 9:6

Whoso sheddeth man's blood,

by man shall his blood be shed:

for in the image of God made he man.

Deuteronomy 1:13

Take you wise men, and understanding,

and known among your tribes,

and I will make them rulers over you.

Proverbs 8:15, 16

By me kings reign, and princes decree justice.

By me princes rule, and nobles,

even all the judges of the earth.

Daniel 2:21

And he changeth the times and the seasons:

he removeth kings, and setteth up kings:

he giveth wisdom unto the wise,

and knowledge to them that know understanding.

Romans 13:1, 2

Let every soul be subject

unto the higher powers.

For there is no power but of God:

the powers that be are ordained of God.

Whosoever therefore resisteth the power,

resisteth the ordinance of God:

and they that resist

shall receive to themselves damnation.

ENGLISH STANDARD VERSION
ASSIGNMENT 12

GOD ESTABLISHED HUMAN GOVERNMENT

Genesis 9:6

"Whoever sheds the blood of man,

by man shall his blood be shed,

for God made man in his own image."

Deuteronomy 1:13

"Choose for your tribes wise, understanding,

and experienced men,

and I will appoint them as your heads."

Proverbs 8:15, 16

By me kings reign, and rulers decree what is just;

by me princes rule, and nobles,

all who govern justly.

Daniel 2:21

He changes times and seasons;

he removes kings and sets up kings;

he gives wisdom to the wise

and knowledge to those who have understanding.

Romans 13:1, 2

Let every person be subject

to the governing authorities.

For there is no authority except from God,

and those that exist have been instituted by God.

Therefore whoever resists the authorities

resists what God has appointed,

and those who resist

will incur judgment.

HELPS AND EXPLANATIONS

Genesis 9:6

Following the great flood, God established human government and gave the human governors the highest power and authority over other men when He said, "Whoso sheddeth man's blood, by man shall his blood be shed." This means that if someone murders a person, the human governors should take the murderer's life. This is capital punishment. God established it so that it would restrain violence in the land.

Deuteronomy 1:13

God instructed Moses to take men of good judgment and understanding, who had good records among their people, and set them up as rulers. This was another step in the way God established human government.

Proverbs 8:15,16

"Decree" – order, deal out.

This is a very enlightening statement. God tells us that, really, in the end it is by His authority that kings reign, it is by His authority that princes rule and deal out justice, and it is by His authority that nobles and judges rule the earth.

We must, therefore, believe that the rulers, the judges and the policemen in our country today, though elected or appointed by other men, yet, in the end, they exercise their powers by the authority of God.

Daniel 2:21

God made time. God made the sun, moon and stars which measure time. He made the day and night and the seasons of the year. This same God can turn night into day. He can make the sun go backward or stand still as in the days of Ahaz and Joshua. He can change times. God is in complete control of the realms of nature which so much rule our lives.

God is also in control of the earthly rulers. He removes kings and sets up kings. He sets up presidents and rulers. He gives wisdom and knowledge to those who really desire it. How important it is, therefore, that Christians really pray for their rulers in order that those in authority might look to God for wisdom in all the great decisions that they have to make from day to day.

Romans 13: 1, 2

"Ordained" – set up, constituted.

"Resisteth" – rebels against.

"Ordinance" – appointment, arrangement.

"Damnation" – judgment, sentence.

"*Let every soul be subject unto the higher powers.*" This means simply and directly that every individual is to be obedient to the ruling authorities in the city, in the state and in the nation.

"*The powers that be are ordained of God.*" Even though we elect people to places of authority and power, the Scriptures state clearly that no authority exists apart from God, and that the powers and rulers, which are over us now, have in fact, been set up and appointed by God. Think it through. This is strong language, but this is God's Word. Much of

our violence, disorder and disobedience to civil authorities today is due to the fact that people do not seem to realize that human government is established by God and that it is under God's control. Some of these things we do not fully understand, but, nevertheless, they are true.

"*Whosoever therefore resisteth the power, resisteth the ordinance of God.*" This means that the person who rebels against the civil authorities in his community or in his country is really resisting the appointment and the arrangement of God. This is God's Word! This was really *something* for the Apostle Paul to write when he was thrown in jail again and again by the civil governments because he preached the gospel. But, you see, Paul wrote these words by inspiration of God, and even though he suffered much at the hands of civil governments, yet he recognized that these words were true.

"*And they that resist shall receive to themselves damnation.*" They that rebel against and resist the powers of government shall receive the sentence and punishment inflicted by the rulers of the land.

Circumstances in which rulers overstep their authority, and in which sometimes it becomes necessary for the servants of God to say, "We must obey God rather than man" (Acts 5:20-29), are not in view in this passage of Scripture.

SCRIPTURE INDEX

CHRISTIAN FOCUS PUBLICATIONS

Christian Focus | Christian Heritage | CF4K | Mentor

Christian Focus Publications publishes books for adults and children under its four main imprints: Christian Focus, Christian Heritage, CF4K and Mentor. Our books reflect that God's word is reliable and Jesus is the way to know him, and live for ever with him.

Our children's publication list includes a Sunday school curriculum that covers pre-school to early teens; puzzle and activity books. We also publish personal and family devotional titles, biographies and inspirational stories that children will love.

If you are looking for quality Bible teaching for children then we have an excellent range of Bible story and age specific theological books.

From pre-school to teenage fiction, we have it covered!

Find us at our web page:
www.christianfocus.com

CF4 •K
*Because you're never
too young to know Jesus*